The need to know guide to life with a toddler and a newborn

How to prepare for and cope with the day to day challenge of raising two young children

NICOLA COOPER-ABBS

Discover more books and ebooks of interest to you and find out about the range of work we do at the forefront of health, fitness and wellbeing.

www.centralymcaguides.com

Published by Central YMCA Trading Ltd (trading as YMCAed).
Registered Company No. 3667206.

Central YMCA is the world's founding YMCA. Established in 1844 in Central London, it was the first YMCA to open its doors and, in so doing, launched a movement that has now grown to become the world's biggest youth organisation. Today, Central YMCA is the UK's leading health, fitness and wellbeing charity, committed to helping people from all walks of life – and particularly the young and those with a specific need – to live happier, healthier and more fulfilled lives.

ISBN: 1482326507
ISBN-13: 978-1482326505

CONTENTS

ABOUT THE AUTHOR

 My name is Nicola Cooper-Abbs and I was born in a small northern town in the 1970s. I'm fairly sure I came out clutching a pencil and pen and asking where the nearest library was. Predictably, I grew up to be writer, studying journalism at the University of Central Lancashire and then moving over to the world of marketing and PR. I spent a couple of years working in an agency, had a quick pit stop in New Zealand and taught English in the exotic location of Salford. Ten years ago I set up as a freelance writer and marketer.

I now spend my time writing about a variety of parenting topics combined with my role as Marketing Director of MumPanel, a specialist insight consultancy. But my most important job is being mum to my two chatty, hilarious and truly wonderful girls.

Central YMCA Mums' Health Guides

INTRODUCTION

I still remember the thrill of finding out I was pregnant, a sense of excitement and trepidation. Wondering if I'd be a good mum and whether my future child would inherit my short legs, their dad's sense of humour or the famous family nose. When I found out I was pregnant with my second child I felt all those emotions again, but there was something else, a very slight sense of panic. You see, I knew what was coming. The toddler in front of me was evidence I had survived it intact, but I wondered how on earth I would cope with a newborn. The sleepless nights, the nappy changes, the hours it took to get out of the door, all that combined with a toddler who demanded every ounce of my patience and minute of my time.

Once again, I did survive. But at the time I would have welcomed an easy-to-digest book with some top hints and tips on the areas I really struggled with – things I often felt too embarrassed to ask friends or the health visitor about. And this is how this book was born. It is designed to be a very practical guide to coping with a toddler and a newborn, from when you are pregnant and preparing for the early days just after birth, until your newborn is a few months old.

Central YMCA Mums' Health Guides

HOW TO USE THIS BOOK

This book is great for sleep-deprived mums and dads who want practical, day-to-day advice from other mums and dads. This isn't a heavy duty guide laden with expert opinions, but everyday hints and tips from other parents, gathered from my own experience and the hundreds of mums I've spoken to since I became a parent and began working for a specialist mum-marketing and insight consultancy. This book is packed full of parent 'insider' information that will make those early days a little less stressful and a lot more enjoyable.

The book is broken down into seven chapters, from organising yourself before your newborn arrives in Chapter One to caring for yourself after the birth in Chapter Two, handling feeding in Chapter Three and keeping your toddler occupied in Chapter Four. Chapter Five covers getting out of the house with a toddler and a newborn, including discussions on double buggies and slings, and Chapter Six looks at scheduling or going with the flow. We finish (as the day does in most homes) with bath and bedtime. In each chapter you'll find handy hints from other mums and in-depth real-life stories which will help you navigate the first few months.

Welcome to being a parent of two!

Central YMCA Mums' Health Guides

1

PREPARING FOR A NEW ARRIVAL

PARENTING TRENDS FOR 2013: This year will see the arrival of a royal baby so you can guarantee parenting is going to be a hot topic. No doubt we'll see a full analysis of how Kate and William parent from what baby gear they choose to whether or not Kate breastfeeds. Expect the shops to follow whatever trends our future king and queen set.

TOP 5 COPING TIPS

1. Shop smart. This time around you know what is essential and what is nice-to-have. You also know how quickly babies grow out of things so stock up on essentials and let friends and relatives spend on the cute outfits.
2. If you want to make changes in your older child's life – perhaps moving them from a cot to a bed, or potty training, then do it well in advance of the new baby coming.
3. If making changes doesn't go according to plan (your toddler would rather pee on the floor than a potty), then just let it go. The stress isn't worth it and you could end up creating more problems than the ones you are attempting to solve. Revisit any decisions to make changes once your newborn is three months old.
4. Everything you can do to help your toddler prepare for their new brother or sister will help. If you can, take them to scans so they can see the new baby, explain what is happening and why it's a good thing; constantly reassure them that your love for them will

not change. Find ways to include them in your preparation for the baby.

5. Ask for help and if it's offered take it. Use the time beforehand to think about what you will need once the baby has arrived and give people jobs to do. You'll find most friends and family are desperate to help in some way.

WHAT TO DO BEFORE BABY ARRIVES

Before you had your first baby you may well have had the luxury of a few weeks off before the birth and plenty of time to prepare. This time you have a bit more to contend with, but you do have a lot more knowledge. The main conclusion most mums come to after number one is that they spent far too much money on useless baby gear that was hardly used. So this is your chance to be a bit more savvy.

☐ Stock up on the essentials – babygros, new bottles and teats if you are bottle-feeding (for hygiene reasons teats should be replaced every 2-3 months), newborn size nappies and a new mattress for the cot/Moses basket. Leave shopping for fancy blankets and outfits to friends and family. A good idea is to ask people for vouchers so you can spend as and when you need to on both children.

☐ Borrow if you can – remember some items will only be used for a few weeks.

☐ Reuse – if you have a pram and car seat from the first time around then they can be rescued, even if they are a bit grubby. A top tip from one mum is to use a jet washer to remove the worst of the grime. Removable covers can be washed and some mums recommend Napisan for cleaning down covers that can't be taken off.

☐ Prepare – get the house clean and organised. Stock up the fridge and freezer with easy to prepare meals.

☐ Make sure your toddler knows the person who will care for them when you give birth – introduce people such as grandparents and build up that bond beforehand.

I'M GETTING A NEW BROTHER OR SISTER?

Your older child is about to have their lovely little universe upset. So far, all they know is that they are the most important person in the world to mummy and daddy and they have had your undivided attention since day one. The arrival of a small, screaming baby is bound to throw them. This new person will suddenly be taking all of mum's attention, they won't be the baby of the family anymore and they'll rightly feel a bit miffed.

Before baby arrives do everything you can to prepare your older child for the arrival and make it as 'real' as possible – take them to scan appointments so they can see the baby, get them to talk to their new brother or sister and ask them to help you choose baby names (my younger child has a middle name chosen by her older sister, although we decided not to go with her first choice, Cheesus). This is also the time to explain that your feelings for your toddler won't change and love is an expandable thing. You are likely to need to keep reinforcing and reassuring your toddler about their place in the family. Be aware though that toddlers don't have a concept of time, so don't tell them too much too early.

Rather than a new arrival making your toddler feel pushed out you can do small things that can make them feel they have the most important job in the world – being a big brother or sister. Depending on the age of your toddler there are good picture books which explain what happens when mummies have babies.

Bright idea: Buy a present from the baby for your toddler. This can be given when the baby arrives (who will be receiving lots of gifts) and ensures you toddler doesn't feel left out.

COT TO BED, NAPPY TO POTTY

The imminent arrival of a second child often prompts parents to make changes such as transitioning from a cot to a bed, or potty training. I asked mums for their views on helping your older child move smoothly through these changes:

- Only attempt what they are ready for. The average age for potty training is between two and three. The older they are the more likely you are to succeed with any changes.
- Leave yourself plenty of time. Don't try to change a toddler from a cot to a bed a week before baby arrives. You need to give them a chance to be happy with the change before more changes happen.
- If your toddler doesn't respond well to the change then revisit it in a couple of months (one good reason to leave plenty of time to try things). If you are close to birth then leave any planned changes until your baby is at least 12 weeks old and you have found your feet.

☐ If you want to move a toddler to a bed, don't forget that baby is likely to be in the same room as you at first, so you may not immediately need your older child's cot. Depending on how much of an escape artist your child is you may want to consider a bed barrier and stair gate.

I NEED HELP!

Most mums find when they are pregnant or have a newborn that they get endless offers of help. And most mums aren't very good at accepting this help. There is no prize for being a supermum, but it can be very hard to accept offers of help when you are put on the spot. So sit down for an hour and think about practical ways people could help you.

Do you need someone to dig out your pram and wash it? Could someone bring round a home cooked meal the first day you are back from hospital? What are your plans for your toddler in the first few days after giving birth? Could someone take them on a special day out somewhere? If your toddler is at preschool or nursery who could take them when you are heavily pregnant or have a newborn? Or could someone sit with your newborn so you can take your toddler to the park for an hour. If you have this list then when someone offers, you can very politely ask them if they can do a particular job.

GIVING BIRTH

As part of your preparation for the arrival of number two it's a good idea to explain to your toddler that mummy might be away for a few days. This is also the time to explain to your toddler that you might not be able to pick them up for a few days (especially important if you have a caesarean section).

And this is also a vital time to prepare yourself. Remember, if you had a difficult birth last time, it doesn't mean that the same thing will happen this time around. I had two radically different births.

If you didn't like how things panned out last time then consider writing up a birth plan that makes your wishes clear.

MUM'S THE WORD...

'I like to be prepared so, as boring as it may be to some, we've found out the sex of our second baby, although we didn't with our first. This is so we know if we were keeping clothes for the new baby or giving them away. As it happens, it's another boy!

We will be moving our first child into a new bedroom and decorating two months beforehand and we hope to tackle potty training before March, when I'm due. We talk to our firstborn about the baby and explain how he is in my tummy, just like he was. He kisses my tummy and says hello. Other preparation has included washing the pram as it has been in the garage.

This time I feel a lot more relaxed – well, at the moment I do!'

Rhiannon, currently pregnant and mum to Alexander, 2.

Central YMCA Mums' Health Guides

2

THE EARLY DAYS

> **PARENTING TRENDS FOR 2013:** Ever wondered what it would be like to have a little Thunder running around your house? Fancy yelling out, 'Thor, put your coat back on,' across the playground? If you haven't yet chosen a name for your newborn then perhaps you could choose from the names predicted to be favoured this year, inspired by climate change and ancient gods.

TOP 5 COPING TIPS

1. Don't expect too much; do you remember the first three months after your first baby? Expect a similar adjustment period.
2. If someone offers help then take it, don't try to be a hero (there are no mum medals up for grabs!).
3. It's OK to feel overwhelmed or resentful of your toddler or newborn – you don't necessarily have to tell anyone you feel that way, but recognising your own feelings and accepting them as normal is a good thing.
4. If you didn't manage to make all the changes or transitions before baby arrived (cot to bed for toddler, potty training etc.) then don't even think about attempting them in the first three months. They will wait and you will hang onto your sanity.
5. Remember that your toddler is a still a baby. All they have ever known is you (and just you, not some stinky, noisy baby and you) so they need as much care and attention as your newborn.

THE FIRST FEW DAYS

Whether you are in hospital, at home, following a caesarean section or a simple, straightforward birth, give yourself time to recover. Forget the superhuman act and take it easy in the first few days. If there is help on hand then use it. The first 36 hours after birth should consist of you resting as much as possible, establishing breastfeeding and introducing your toddler to their sister or brother. That's more than enough for the average mum to cope with!

MUMMY YOU STINK!

You might find in the initial few days after you give birth that your toddler doesn't want to cuddle you or be near you. Although this might be down to feeling pushed out by the new baby it can also be due to the way you look and smell. From a child's point of view they have watched your body change radically over a period of a few months and then almost overnight your bump disappears and your boobs become enormous. For a child, sudden changes in appearance can be unsettling. Combine that with the fact that, due to hormones, postnatal bleeding and breastfeeding, you may smell very different. It's not at all unusual for your older child to react to this in quite a negative way. The best course of action is reassurance and, if they are old enough, to explain to your toddler why your body has changed.

MAKING INTRODUCTIONS

Most toddlers will happily accept a baby brother or sister and most parents are aware of the need to help their toddler through this period of change. There are a few things you can do to make the transition easier.

- ☐ After you have given birth make sure your older child comes to hospital and meets their new brother or sister. Make it a fun outing with lots of attention paid to your toddler (and a great time to hand over the presents that the new baby has bought).
- ☐ Ask people who are coming to see the baby to make a fuss of your toddler as well. Your toddler will want to know they are still important in people's lives.
- ☐ Encourage bonding between your toddler and newborn. While carefully supervised, get them to hold the baby, gently stroke his or her face or hold their fingers.
- ☐ It's an old wives' tale that the first meeting determines how siblings will get on, so if it doesn't go according to plan, don't panic.

☐ Explain to your toddler what a baby needs when it cries and how you will deal with it.

☐ It's normal to feel very protective of your newborn, but don't tell your older child off if they are a bit over-excited around your baby. Instead, re-direct their behaviour to something positive: 'How about you stroke the baby's face', 'Do you think he needs some milk?' Obviously, it's vital that you teach a toddler to be gentle, but you should encourage their exploration rather than tell them off.

☐ Behaviour such as poking and grabbing is quite normal. If your toddler sees you reacting to this then they have just what they want – your attention. Try to ensure your toddler is getting lots of positive attention so they feel less inclined to carry out negative attention-seeking acts.

POSTNATAL DEPRESSION

Postnatal depression is incredibly common with an estimated one in seven women suffering from it in the three months following birth. In the days after birth it's normal to feel tearful and a bit blue. If these feelings don't start to get better after a few weeks and you continue to feel low, have trouble sleeping or feel you can't cope then you may have developed postnatal depression.

The most important thing to remember is that postnatal depression is a recognised, and in most cases, easily treatable illness. It does not make you a bad mother, it does not mean you don't love your children and you will not have your children taken away if you tell someone. Most midwives or health visitors carry out a questionnaire to check how you are feeling but you can always approach them to talk through things. Your GP can also help. If you don't feel you can talk to a health professional then try and tell a friend, family member or partner how you feel so they can support you as you find the help you need. Postnatal depression can be treated with medication, self-help or therapy.

BACK TO WORK

For many mums the day their partner returns to work after paternity leave is their lowest point. Juggling a toddler and a newborn is easier when you have two pairs of hands, but there are some practical ways you can make days less stressful.

☐ Ask your partner to do shorter days when they first go back. Knowing someone is coming home an hour or two earlier can make the day a lot easier.

☐ This is the time to take up all of the offers of help. Ask someone to sit with your newborn so you can take your toddler to the park. Get someone to pop around so you can have a shower in peace at least once a week. If people come to visit and ask what they can do give them a practical task – put a load of washing on, get some basic shopping.

☐ Don't try and do it all at once. Forget running around and cleaning, spend the time you have adjusting to being a bigger family and helping your children bond.

☐ Whenever you can, make your life easier – organize online shopping so you don't have to drag two children around the supermarket, forget home cooked meals for a week or two.

☐ When your partner gets home at the end of the day take some time for you. Do whatever relaxes you, from reading a book to going for a run (or sleeping!). Let your partner take over for a while.

Bright idea: Although the advice is always to sleep when baby sleeps this is almost impossible when you have a toddler. Instead, create a space in the day for quiet time when you sit together and read a book or watch a movie.

DAY-TO-DAY JUGGLE

Once you have got over the first few days then it's time to tackle the fact that you only have one pair of hands. Many mums feel overwhelmed at first because they suddenly have two people and two sets (of often conflicting) needs to deal with.

☐ It's OK to feel overwhelmed and to wonder whether you can cope – you will, but getting used to the demands of two little people takes time. We all know that feeling guilty is a part of parenting and this can be magnified after number two comes along. The fact that you even feel guilty is a good sign – it means you care about the welfare of your children, but don't let it consume you; babies can be left to cry for short periods, toddlers can wait 10 minutes for their tea. Be realistic and accept that things will be different – parenting isn't about being perfect.

☐ Find your coping mechanisms. They'll be different for everyone but here are some that mums have told me about:

- ☐ I used to have baby in a swing and toddler playing on the bathroom floor so I could take a shower.

- ☐ I'd get both of mine doing things at the same time, so teatime for toddler was also feeding time for baby. Bath time was together – at least that way I wasn't doing everything twice!

- ☐ Although I used to hate hearing it, I did sometimes leave my baby to cry to deal with my toddler. My instinct was always to run to my younger child but I soon realised my toddler needed me just as much and I knew from the first time around that babies can cry and be OK.

- ☐ For me a sling was a lifesaver, hands free to deal with my toddler and a content baby.

- ☐ I forgot everything I said I 'should do' – I used CBeebies and television when I needed to, I gave a dummy to the baby, I took two minutes out in the garden to breathe when I needed to.

- ☐ Sometimes I shouted and that's OK – it didn't make me a bad mum. I always made sure I apologised to my toddler.

- ☐ Don't compare yourself to other mums and what they are 'achieving' – it will always make you feel bad.

- ☐ If people offer help, take it, even if they aren't your favourite person! If you can afford it then pay for help, having cleaners and my elder in preschool for a few hours a week was a godsend.

- ☐ Remember that you have just produced a lifelong buddy for your older child – that's a worth a few weeks of chaos.

CO-SLEEPING

Some people choose to sleep with their toddler or baby (or both). This is known as co-sleeping. If you have been co-sleeping with your toddler and want to move them to a cot or bed then any transition should have started when you were pregnant.

It is possible to co-sleep with both a toddler and baby, but there are some important safety guidelines that should be followed. Indeed, it should also be noted that the NHS in the UK advises that 'the safest place for your baby to sleep for the first six months is in a cot in a room with you'.

If you do wish to co-sleep please bear the following NHS advice in mind:

Don't share a bed with your baby if you or your partner:

☐ are smokers (no matter where or when you smoke and even if you never smoke in bed)

☐ have recently drunk alcohol

☐ have taken medication or drugs that make you sleep more heavily

☐ feel very tired

The risks of bed sharing are also increased if your baby:

☐ was premature (born before 37 weeks), or

☐ was of low birth weight (less than 2.5kg or 5.5lb)

There's also a risk that you might roll over in your sleep and suffocate your baby. Or your baby could get caught between the wall and the bed, or roll out of an adult bed and be injured.

(Source: http://www.nhs.uk/Conditions/pregnancy-and-baby/Pages/getting-baby-to-sleep.aspx#close)

MUM'S THE WORD...

'I have a 13 month gap between my two boys. It's been a lot better than I thought; most people said we were crazy having two so close. I think keeping feeds for baby regular helps, and just accept as much help as possible.

'We were very lucky to have parents close by who were able to help with the practical things on a regular basis such as taking my older one out to keep him occupied or feeding my younger one so I could spend time with his big brother. My main problem was finding a baby bag big enough for all the stuff I now need to carry, there is so much!'

Hayley, mum to Joshua (18 months) and Harry (4 and half months old).

3

FEEDING TIME

PARENTING TRENDS FOR 2013: If you believe everything you read in the papers then we are in for a serious baby boom this year thanks to one book. Yes, that's right; it's the *Fifty Shades of Grey* phenomenon. And with 40 million copies sold worldwide, that's an awful lot of sleepless nights and nappy changes to come.

TOP 5 COPING TIPS

1. It can be confusing for a toddler to see you breastfeeding if they have never experienced it – take the time to explain that's where babies get their food.
2. Be aware that between having babies (even if they are very close together) that guidelines around feeding, making up bottles, sleeping and other baby-related information may have changed. Make sure you read information from your midwife or health visitor.
3. Find ways to get your toddler involved in feeding, from bringing you a muslin to having a special book you read when nursing.
4. Feeding can be a great time to spend some quiet, close bonding time with both of your children.
5. It is possible to breastfeed two children at the same time; this is known as tandem nursing.

FEEDING TIME

If you have chosen to breastfeed your newborn then you may need some practical tips to cope with an active toddler and the feeding demands of your baby.

If your child is a little older and weaned or you didn't breastfeed the first time around then first take the time to explain that breast milk is food for the baby and that breastfeeding can also be used for comfort.

- ☐ Don't try to hide breastfeeding from your toddler, they will be curious, and it's a beautiful, nurturing behaviour to show to your child.
- ☐ If your toddler is still breastfeeding then you may need assistance to establish tandem nursing – a specialist breastfeeding midwife should be able to help.
- ☐ Get your older child involved by asking them to bring you blankets or get you a water bottle.
- ☐ If you are struggling with breastfeeding then do seek help – the National Breastfeeding Helpline is a good place to start. But don't feel guilty if breastfeeding doesn't work out for you.
- ☐ It's very common for toddlers suddenly to want to breastfeed again – you can either let them (most just mess around!) or distract them with another activity such as drinking from a special sippy cup.
- ☐ With practice you can breastfeed one handed, using a small rolled up towel to support your breast, leaving you with one free hand to cuddle your toddler or carry out an activity with them.
- ☐ Breastfeeding cafés and groups are a great place to drop in and pick up tips from other mums such as breastfeeding using a sling or lying down – both of which give you a bit more freedom to deal with your toddler.
- ☐ Have activities set up for during breastfeeding sessions – this could be anything from Lego to drawing books to a short burst of television. There is more advice on keeping your toddler occupied in Chapter Four.

EXPRESSING

Expressing is when you squeeze milk out of your breasts, by hand or using a pump, so you can store it and use it later. You might choose to do this so your partner can also share feeding duties. If you are going back to work you may want to express so your baby continues to have the benefits of breast milk. Most breastfeeding experts say if you want to continue breastfeeding successfully you should hold off introducing a bottle until baby is about one month old and breastfeeding is well established.

WHO GUIDELINES ON BREASTFEEDING

The World Health Organization recommends that all mothers (globally) breastfeed exclusively for the first six months for 'optimal growth, development and health'.

Bright idea: If you are breastfeeding out and about then it can be a good idea to keep your toddler in a highchair or pushchair so they can't bolt the minute your baby latches on.

MAKING UP BOTTLES – CURRENT GUIDELINES

One of the biggest surprises I got when my younger girl was born was that the guidelines for making up bottles had completely changed. It's tempting to ignore any new information and keep doing things the way you always have because your older child was fine. However, new information becomes known because research is on-going and the findings can save your child's life.

The current advice is that you should make up each feed as your baby needs it. There is a very good reason for doing this. Even when a formula tin or packet is sealed it can still contain bacteria such as Salmonella. This type of bacteria is rare, but if your baby was to get an infection caused by this bug it can be life threatening.

So you should therefore sterilise all bottles and teats before making a feed, and wash your hands thoroughly. Fill the kettle with fresh water, boil and then make your feed (the water must be at least 70 degrees). If the feed is too hot you can cool it by running the bottom half of the bottle under cold water. If you leave made up bottles on the side or in the fridge then any bacteria can multiply, that's why making each bottle up when needed is safest. Your midwife or health visitor can give you more advice on making up bottles safely. You can also find guidelines on the NHS website here:

www.nhs.uk/Conditions/pregnancy-and-baby/Pages/bottle-feeding-advice.aspx

MUM'S THE WORD...

'Feeding a newborn and a toddler can be demanding, as invariably in the early days they will have very different feeding schedules. And of course, you need to feed yourself as well! I coped with this by making a list of simple meals and sticking it to the hob, to remind myself of quick and easy things I could make that myself and Sebastian would enjoy, and that were also easy to prepare with a newborn in a baby sling.

'Sometimes I was lucky and Daphne would be sleeping whilst I needed to make his lunch or tea, but inevitably there will always be times where the newborn wants to be held and the toddler wants food. And 'easy to prepare' includes the proviso 'not requiring use of the hob or oven' since both of those things would potentially mean putting a baby in a sling precariously close to intense heat. So anything microwaveable is great. Jacket potatoes with cheese, or tuna, for example. Toast with beans. Hot dogs.

Also, if you have the time, perhaps at weekends if someone else is around to help, it's great to make a huge stash of reheatable meals like lasagne, fish pie etc., split into toddler and mummy size portions in the freezer and then they're all ready to put in the microwave! And if all else fails, have a supply of breadsticks and yoghurts on standby. In my experience, most toddlers are happy with breadsticks and yoghurt.'

Lauren, mum to Sebastian (3 and a half) and Daphne (16 months). Blogger at www.mummyisagadgetgeek.co.uk

4

KEEPING YOUR TODDLER OCCUPIED

PARENTING TRENDS FOR 2013: In 2012 we saw baby showers becoming more popular in the UK, but this year we might just see the rise of something more focussed on fathers – the **Dadchelor party – it's a chance for dad to have one last hurrah with his friends before baby arrives and sleep deprivation takes over.**

TOP 5 COPING TIPS

1. Toddlers have a unique ability to get themselves into all kinds of mischief when you aren't watching – create safe spaces where you know you can leave them for a few minutes.

2. Make your toddler the most important person by giving them tasks and then telling them what a good job they are doing.

3. Use positive language: 'I can see you want to play with your sister,' rather than, 'Stop poking your sister.' Learn to redirect bad behaviour rather than tackle every minor problem.

4. Think about what keeps your child occupied for longest – from books to TV programmes – and use it. Until you find your routine you will need the time it gives you.

5. Toddlers often want to be babies again when a brother or sister appears on the scene; this is quite normal and usually disappears after a few weeks.

TODDLER CHAOS

It doesn't really matter whether your toddler is one or three when the newborn arrives; at any age they are likely to require a great deal of attention and care. Here are some tips for keeping your toddler occupied, whether you just need two minutes for a shower or time to make a phone call.

A word of caution. Toddlers can be terrors and find a million ways of injuring themselves or ingesting something they shouldn't the minute your back is turned. It hardly needs saying, but never leave your child unattended for long periods of time and carry out basic baby proofing in your house such as stair gates, cupboard locks and putting medicines out of reach.

YOUR LITTLE HELPER

One of the most powerful tools in your parenting kit when you have a toddler and a newborn is to make your toddler your assistant. Getting them involved in caring for your newborn strengthens the bond between siblings, ensures they don't feel left out and gives you an opportunity to have lots of positive interaction with them. It can also be very useful to have a spare pair of hands. They can do simple things like bring you baby wipes and it can give you valuable minutes when you need to sort out baby. Children love to feel important and valued, and here are a few ways you can get them involved:

- Get them to bring you wipes or nappies during a change.
- Ask them to take things to the bin for you.
- Encourage them to choose toys, books and clothes for your newborn. Every time they do something for you reinforce what a great job they are doing.
- Get them to hold hands with the baby or stroke their arm when they need comforting (this might be at the same time you are cuddling).
- If your child is old enough and you are bottle-feeding, with supervision, get them to feed the baby (if they are younger then it might be their job to give the baby a dummy or blanket).
- Find games that involve and appeal to your toddler but can be played by both, such as peekaboo.
- Show your older child that the baby wants them around by talking about what the baby is doing: 'Look, he's reaching out for your hand,' or 'She's watching you playing.'

- ☐ Appoint your toddler as 'chief rocker' with responsibility for rocking your crying newborn in their car seat or crib when they're grizzling.
- ☐ Encourage your toddler to sing to the baby when they're crying, and make sure you sing along too so that it's a joint effort to settle the little one.

USING THE RIGHT LANGUAGE

When you are stressed it can be difficult to stay calm around your toddler. Using positive language and encouragement rather than shouting commands can help to create a calmer home environment and show your toddler they don't have to behave badly to get your attention. It might feel strange at first, but try to acknowledge how your toddler feels: 'It must make you mad because the baby is taking up all of mummy's attention.' Sometimes all we need (even when we are two) is for our feelings to be recognised. It's a good idea to go easy on the discipline with your toddler in the first few weeks as they go through the changes in the family. Choose your battles and learn when to let things go.

Bright idea: Always have a drink and snack ready for your toddler before baby feeds and changes as they will want one as soon as you sit down.

TODDLER TIME

You are the centre of the universe for your toddler and the more you can be there for them the less likely you will encounter tantrums or a negative reaction against the baby.

- ☐ Create a toddler friendly room or space, with a stair gate, so you can go the toilet or take a shower knowing they are safe.
- ☐ Gather a collection of toys that your toddler will play with that don't require constant intervention by you.
- ☐ Technology can be incredibly useful – so have favourite DVDs or computer games that can be used during feeding time.
- ☐ If you need to sleep, create a safe sleeping place in a room your toddler can't escape from.
- ☐ Create time in each day just for your toddler; this can be hard when you are tired, but it's worth it to make your older child feel secure.

☐ Have a toddler box, packed full of toys and books which are specifically for when you are nursing. This can be changed every few days so your toddler doesn't get bored.

☐ Tell your toddler stories – about when they were a newborn, the funny things they did when they were growing up and what they can do now they are a 'big boy or girl'.

☐ Find what keeps your toddler occupied and use it – mums have told us that the things that kept their toddlers occupied (age dependent) were role playing (feeding like mummy), play dough, painting and looking through photographs.

DEVELOPMENT AND GOING BACKWARDS

When your newborn arrives you might see your toddler regress, a potty-trained child might suddenly start peeing on the floor. Regression is very normal and can include baby talk, wanting to wear nappies, use a dummy or be carried. It's best to allow some of this behaviour while reinforcing all the things big girls or boys get to do. Most toddlers adjust after a few weeks and get back on track. If they don't and you have any concerns then speak to your GP or health visitor.

DAD'S THE WORD...

'Probably the most important thing I did as a dad when our second baby arrived was to become my older child's best buddy. I'd go straight to her when I came in from work and ask about what she'd been up to. At the weekends I would always make time to take my older child to the park or on little outings, which she loved. They were often simple things like going on a bus or to the cinema but it was our special time. My bonding time with my newborn was first thing in the morning or during a night feed.'

Ian, dad to Mia (6) and Lily (3)

5

GETTING OUT OF THE HOUSE

PARENTING TRENDS FOR 2013: Last year neon clothes made a serious come back and every child of the 80s suddenly felt right at home again. This year that fashion trend is making its way into the world of babies. Instead of hues of pink and blue you'll see prams and buggies featuring flashes of bright neon yellow, pink and green.

TOP 5 COPING TIPS

1. You have several options when it comes to transporting two, but if you can't decide which will work for you then hire or borrow some kit for a few weeks.
2. As soon as you can, get out of the house; you, baby and toddler will benefit from seeing other people and having a bit of fresh air.
3. Sling libraries are a good place to hire and try out different types of slings, which are a great way to keep babies calm and your hands free for toddlers.
4. If you need a double buggy then think lifestyle – where will you use it? Will it fit in your car and your house? This will start to determine the right pram for you.
5. Don't be tempted to put a toddler in a car seat that isn't really suitable. Find a retailer who will talk to you about the right kind of seats and try different ones out for a perfect fit.

TRANSPORTING A BABY AND A TODDLER

Depending on the age of your toddler you have the following options:

- ☐ Double buggy (tandem or twin)
- ☐ Pram and buggy board
- ☐ Pram/sling and walking child (reins an option)
- ☐ Pram and sling

What suits you will depend on how much time you spend in a car or walking, how old and obliging your toddler is (will they walk or stand on a buggy board) and what you have the budget to do. It can be a good idea to hire or borrow a sling, double pram and buggy board to find out which combination works best for you.

AND BREATHE!

The universal advice from all mums is, as soon as you possibly can, get out of the house. For most mums a bit of fresh air and a chance for your toddler to run around is a sanity-saver. You don't have to walk for miles, but it is a great way to settle a cranky newborn and for you to see something other than your familiar four walls.

DAILY CHORES

If you have daily chores or regular outings that need doing as soon as your newborn arrives, such as preschool or nursery drop off, then make sure you have arranged cover for doing this. If you have a tricky birth you may not be able to drive or walk very far, so pre-planning who will help in the first few days can take a lot of stress away. One tip I hear from mums time and time again is to prepare your changing bag the night before rather than rushing to do it in the morning. And always have spares for both children of clothes, formula, nappies and wipes in your car.

LOWER YOUR EXPECTATIONS

If you cast your mind back to your first you may remember still being in your pyjamas at lunchtime with a rumbling stomach. And that might just happen again! Don't put too much pressure on yourself by arranging things for early in the day or feeling as if you have to look like something that has stepped out of the pages of Vogue.

On the other hand if it makes you feel better to have a shower and do your hair and makeup then check out Chapter Four on keeping your toddler occupied. Here are a few more tips on carrying out day-to-day tasks with two:

- ☐ We all need to take care of the basics – washing and going to the toilet. Create a safe situation for your toddler and baby (toddler playing on bathroom floor, baby in swing) so you can escape for two minutes.
- ☐ Remember hair straighteners, makeup and other cosmetics pose a risk for toddlers. Keep them hidden away if possible.
- ☐ Have a go-to wardrobe of easy to wear, comfortable clothes that require no ironing and no thinking about.
- ☐ If you want to cook around children keep them clear of ovens, sinks and knives. Set them up with a task so you can see them, but they are clear of any hazards. Stick to easy to put together meals for the first few weeks and keep a takeaway menu to hand if it all goes pear-shaped.
- ☐ Online shopping is your saviour, but if you still prefer to go to the supermarket don't go near feeding times. It's worth waiting until the quietest time of the day so supermarket staff are free to give you a hand. Finally, be prepared to abandon ship if a toddler and newborn meltdown happens.

BUT WHERE DO I GO WITH TWO?

There are now hundreds of baby groups across the UK – from NCT meetings to Facebook meet-ups and local church hall groups. Most will welcome a baby and a toddler and they are a cheap way of getting out of the house and meeting other mums. If you don't or can't leave the house then you can find help and support from other mums on parenting forums and websites such as Mumsnet, Netmums and Babycentre.

Sometimes it can take a bit of experimenting to find the right group for you, but they can be great places to forge friendships. Check local notice boards in shops, GP surgeries and your local children's centre for more information.

SLING SAFETY

In the last couple of years there have been concerns raised about the safety of slings and baby wearing. In 2010, a particular type of sling, known as a 'duffel style' sling, was recalled because it was thought to be responsible for the deaths of several babies. This type of sling held babies in a position where it was hard for them to breathe and parents couldn't see them as easily as other styles of sling.

Any sling you buy today should come with advice on how to wear it so your child is safe. In general, the advice is that a sling should hold your baby the way you would hold them in your arms (except for back carriers).

You should always be able to see your baby's face and head without having to move any fabric and they should be able to breathe freely. Your baby's neck should always be in a neutral position and not curled onto their chest. Finally, you should check your baby frequently and adjust their position if needed.

For more information visit this useful link from British consumer champions Which?: www.which.co.uk/baby-and-child/baby-transport/guides/choosing-a-sling-or-baby-carrier/baby-sling-safety

SLING LIBRARIES

As baby wearing and slings have become more popular local sling libraries have popped up all over the UK. These are groups, usually run by a mum with lots of sling knowledge, where you can borrow and try out different styles of slings. They usually charge a small fee for hire and can give advice on the right type of sling for you.

DOUBLE BUGGIES – A BUYING GUIDE

If you've decided that you need a double buggy then here's some advice on what to think about before you make that all important purchase.

There are two types of double buggy: the more traditional side-by-side, often known as a twin, or a more modern tandem buggy where one baby sits in front or above the other. By the time you have your second baby, even if they are very close together, you shouldn't need a buggy that goes flat (designed for twins from birth) but you may still want it to be comfortable enough to sleep in. Depending on the age gap, it might be worth considering a pram that converts back to a single buggy for when your older child wants to walk.

You need to have two things in mind when you go to buy a double buggy – your house and your car. Twin pushchairs are often lighter (and easier to lift into your car) but can be a nightmare if you travel on public transport or have a narrow hallway at home and nowhere to store it (think lifting sleeping babies out!). It's worth tracking down a retailer with a few double buggies and either measuring them or physically trying to get them in your car.

Think about when and how you use your buggy. Will you be using it around town, in and out of shops? If so, a tandem buggy might be a better choice. If you live in a rural area then you might need an off-roader.

Other things to think about:

- ☐ How easy are the straps to adjust and do up? Struggling to get one crying child into a buggy is hard enough, but tricky straps can make getting two of them in a nightmare.
- ☐ Balance and weight. Try out your buggy before committing as a fully laden double buggy is heavier and harder to steer than the single buggy you may be used to. Tandem and twin buggies also feel very different, so go with what you're most confident with.
- ☐ Rain covers. Not all buggies come with one as standard, and many are so badly designed that fitting them is like trying to put a duvet cover on a super king duvet.
- ☐ Foldability. All buggy manufacturers say that their products are easy to fold, but that's not strictly true. No two buggies are the same and what works well for one person may seem like a test on the Krypton Factor for someone else. Test and try before you buy.
- ☐ And don't forget auction sites if you're looking to buy a buggy, you could save hundreds of pounds.

Bright idea: It's worth checking independent reviews from other mums on parenting forums to give you an idea if a particular double buggy might work for you. Another option to consider is hiring a double pushchair to see which style suits you and your family best.

CAR SEATS

When parents are expecting their second child they often think about moving a toddler into a bigger car seat. It can be tempting to buy something off the internet and ditch the five-point harness in favour of a booster. As parents we need to remember that putting a child in a car seat that is the wrong size for them, or doesn't fit properly, is exposing them to unnecessary risk. There are now lots of car seats that keep your child in a five-point harness for longer, ensuring they are not ejected in a car crash. There are retailers who offer a fitting and testing service where you take your car and try different car seats to find the best fit.

REAR-FACING CAR SEATS

In the last few years rear-facing car seats in the UK have become more popular. In the UK when babies outgrow their first rear-facing car seat we usually buy forward-facing car seats. But in other countries parents keep their children in rear-facing car seats until they are five or six. If you were to have a crash a child's neck can be easily damaged as their head is proportionally much heavier than an adult's and they have weaker neck muscles. Rear-facing car seats prevent the head being flung forward and the neck damaged. If you are interested in rear-facing you need to find a specialist retailer as they can be harder to fit than a conventional forward-facing seat.

MUM'S THE WORD...

'I opted for a double pram as it was easier for me to keep an eye on my toddler that way. The other things that worked for me when it came to being a mum of two was to be organised and plan my days – little things like planning my toddler's meals and freezing some so teatimes were a little easier.

'I got my newborn into a sleeping pattern so I could spend time with my toddler and got my partner to help with bath and bedtime so the children got used to someone other than me putting them to bed. I also let my children settle themselves to sleep, it was hard at first with lots of tears from everyone, but it was worth it in the long run as now they both go straight off to sleep when I put them down.'

Barbara, mum to Ruby (2 and a half) and Amber (18 months)

6

SCHEDULE OR GO WITH THE FLOW?

PARENTING TRENDS 2013: This year will see changes to the benefits that UK parents receive, with many high earners no longer receiving child benefit, or seeing reductions in the amount they do receive. Unpaid parental leave will also be extended to 18 weeks in the EU helping to protect working parents who need to look after sick children or relatives. Hopefully we will also see measures that will help parents work flexibly and find ways to cope with the costs of childcare.

TOP 5 COPING TIPS

1. Look at how your life works now and think about whether scheduling is right for you and your family.
2. Think about your own personality and what you prefer – if you don't like routine then trying to follow one could be very stressful.
3. Whether you routine or not doesn't have to be a hard and fast rule – you can combine expert opinion with what works for your family. Remember, what is right for your friends might not work for you and your toddler.
4. Babies do eventually settle into a sort-of routine around 8-12 weeks without any scheduling.
5. There are always new parenting styles and trends popping up and you might be able to take a lot from them, but don't think you have to follow the fashion (and child rearing techniques do go in and out of fashion).

DO I NEED A ROUTINE?

Parents are now bombarded with conflicting information – you need to get your baby on a schedule, you need to feed on demand, you should get your toddler into bed at the same time as your baby, you should let you toddler stay up. What works best for you is a matter of personal choice; there are no hard and fast rules and no-one else can dictate whether sticking to a routine or going with the flow is best for you. However, if you aren't sure what might work for you then here is a quick rundown to help you determine which style of parenting might suit you.

You might prefer a routine if…

☐ Your older child is already in a set routine and it works well for you as a family.

☐ You are a very organised person and like schedules and knowing what is coming (as much as you can with two small children).

☐ You prefer to stick to certain bedtimes and naptimes so you know when you will get a break.

You might prefer going with the flow if…

☐ You didn't follow a schedule the first time and you liked it. Or you did follow a routine and it didn't work for your family.

☐ You don't particularly like routine yourself and don't tend to stick to the same meal or bedtimes.

☐ You prefer the idea of feeding on demand and letting the baby sleep when it suits them.

It's worth keeping in mind that babies have no idea what a routine is, they don't even know the difference between day and night at first. It can be best to wait to get into a routine until they are 8-12 weeks old, when feeding and sleeping patterns start to settle down.

However, sticking to a routine or not doesn't have to be a yes or no choice. There are three different types of routine – parent-led, baby-led and combination. Parent-led is when the parent sets the schedule, sometimes based on baby's patterns but often suggested by an expert. This is usually quite strict, often down to the minute. Baby-led is the other end of the spectrum where you follow your baby's lead, looking out for signs of them being hungry or tired and responding appropriately. That doesn't mean that complete chaos reigns because after a few weeks most babies start to follow their own patterns of feeding and sleeping. In combination, you'll stick to a rough timetable of feeding and sleeping etc. but you will have a greater degree of flexibility.

ATTACHMENT PARENTING

The last few years has seen a growth in a type of parenting style called attachment parenting. The basic idea behind this style is that, by keeping your child close, becoming in tune with them and responding promptly to their needs, you can better meet their emotional and physical requirements. Attachment parenting practices vary, but usually include breastfeeding on demand, using slings rather than prams and co-sleeping. There are a number of websites and groups dedicated to bringing parents together who follow attachment parenting principles.

MUM'S THE WORD...

'Before my son was born I researched routines incorporating both a newborn and a toddler and tailored it to suit our lifestyle and needs. The difference was I started the routine in hospital, where we remained for seven days following his birth. It was tricky at first meeting the demands of a newborn and toddler, but the routine gave a structure to the day which I found incredibly useful when things became overwhelming.

'An important part of our routine is to get out of the house every single day, sometimes to organised groups or classes, a friend's house, the supermarket or just a walk (rain or shine). A good double buggy is essential and an established routine means you can leave the house knowing your newborn won't suddenly start demanding a feed (I won't mention how we completely forgot to feed our daughter before her christening). Having a change bag prepared and already in the car or buggy makes it easier to leave the house. When my newborn was very tiny I tried to go out during his nap times as babies tend to sleep in the car and buggy and extra sleep could mean a wide awake baby at 7pm.

'Notwithstanding all of the above, babies aren't machines and there will be days they laugh in the face of your routine, but tomorrow is always another day and the good days far outweigh the bad.'

Clare, mummy to Gracie 3 and Rafferty 23 months and blogger at www.belfastmummy.co.uk

7

BATH AND BEDTIME

PARENTING TRENDS FOR 2013: If your house is anything like mine it will be bursting at the seams with artwork that your children have created. It can be incredibly hard to part with their first scribbly masterpieces, but storing hundreds of bits of glitter-covered paper can be tricky. This year you can solve that problem by visiting websites like Artkive where you can use your mobile phone to store their artwork electronically and turn it into a book or other keepsake.

TOP 5 COPING TIPS

1. The end of the day is always going to be tricky especially if your baby is colicky and your toddler is tired. Sometimes just recognising this fact can be important – it allows you to be a bit more patient with everyone, including yourself.
2. There is no right way to do bath and bedtime and you need to find what works for you (and it can take a few weeks to figure that out).
3. Your children won't suffer if they don't get a bath every night; a wash down is fine for the days when it all just seems a bit too much.
4. Swings, slings and things that keep toddlers occupied such as books and television are your friends at this time of day.
5. Children cry and you will have bad days. Sometimes you just need to survive those times by doing whatever works (even if it doesn't follow the 'rules').

IT'S THE END OF THE DAY

By the time 5pm rolls around your reserves will be low and instead of a nice relaxing evening you'll probably be experiencing what I lovingly refer to as 'crazy time'. It's that time of the day when everyone is a bit overtired and you need to move through the routine of bath and bedtime with as little stress as possible. Of course, it was quite easy when you had one, but now? Not to worry, as here are some options to make bath and bedtime go without a hitch.

IN THE BATH

- ☐ Try bathing both children at the same time with your toddler in the bath and the baby in a supportive plastic or foam seat. That way you have your hands free to wash your toddler.

- ☐ If bathing both at the same time doesn't suit you or baby needs a feed then sit in the bathroom feeding while your toddler is in the bath. You can always pause briefly (a sling can come in handy here) to get your toddler out and dried. Within a few days you will also develop amazing powers to do many things one-handed.

- ☐ Get baby out of the bath first, wrap them in a towel and put them on another towel or mat. Then get your toddler out and dry.

- ☐ Try and foster independence in your toddler. Teach them to use a flannel to wash their face and hands, show them how to rub shampoo into their hair and dry themselves down with a towel. This, of course, will depend on the age, ability and willingness of your toddler to co-operate. Anything you can do to turn it into a game will help – how foamy can you make your hair, how quickly can you get dressed etc.

- ☐ If baby is sleeping when you want to bathe your older child then bring a bouncy chair or swing into or close to the bathroom.

- ☐ You don't have to bathe at the end of the day (or at all!) – try bathing during the day, first thing in morning, showering or just a good clean down with a flannel. Many mums enjoy bathing or showering as a family.

- ☐ And of course, never leave either child by themselves in or near water.

BEDTIME

- ☐ You'll find your own rhythm and combination of what works for getting your toddler and baby in to bed. This often depends on the personalities of your children (are they screamers or happy kickers content to be left alone?) and the routines and habits you may already have for an older child (do you have to stay with them until they fall asleep? Do they always have a bedtime story?).

- ☐ Try feeding while reading your older child a bedtime story – you can do this on the bed with one child on each side.

- ☐ If your baby naps in the evening, take this opportunity to settle your older child, following their normal routine. If baby wakes up pop them in a sling or swing.

- ☐ If you have an evening screamer or a baby suffering from colic you might have to accept that the evening routine is going to go to pot. If help is available, take it – whether that's a partner dealing with your toddler or a friend or family member who can hold baby while you do bath and bedtime with your toddler a couple of times a week.

- ☐ Many mums find it easier to deal with their toddler and pop baby in their swing or cot for 10 minutes – you know they are safe and secure and can always be occupied with toys or a mobile.

- ☐ The television and other gadgets such as tablets/phones can be your friend at this time of the day. Use them to keep your toddler occupied while you settle the baby.

- ☐ Babies cry. Toddlers cry (and whinge) and you will have to listen to both. They'll be OK and so will you. If all else fails throw all the advice out of the window and opt for survival – this might be decamping to grandma's house, waiting until daddy gets home, going for a drive or a walk, or just all cuddling together on the sofa in your pyjamas.

Bright idea: Find bath products that work for both of your children, then you don't have lots of bottles cluttering up the bathroom. You can usually use the same product for hair washing and bathing.

MUM'S THE WORD...

'I always used to bath Emily (baby) first with help from Maddy. Passing shampoo etc. made her feel involved. Emily loved having Maddy around and they always had smiles for each other. Maddy didn't always have a bath every night as Daddy may have been home early and they had their time together reading or playing. Once Emily was dry, had had her bottle and was in bed, it was reaching 7pm and then Maddy had half an hour to wash her face and of course have a bottle for a while so that she was the same as Emily! A nice story and hug time from mummy and all done.'

Sam, mum to Maddy (7), Emily (5) and Oliver (17 months)

RESOURCES

CHAPTER 1 - PREPARING FOR A NEW ARRIVAL

Parenting forums
www.mumsnet.com
www.netmums.com

The UK's largest charity for parents – antenatal classes and postnatal support
www.nct.org.uk

Sure Start Centres – providing parenting help, support and childcare in your community
www.gov.uk/find-sure-start-childrens-centre

CHAPTER 2 - THE EARLY DAYS

Postnatal depression
www.nhs.uk/conditions/Postnataldepression/Pages/Introduction.aspx

Co-sleeping
www.babycentre.co.uk/a558334/making-co-sleeping-safe

CHAPTER 3 - FEEDING TIME

Tandem breastfeeding
www.llli.org/faq/tandem.html

WHO guidelines on breastfeeding
www.who.int/topics/breastfeeding/en

Making up bottles of formula safely
www.nhs.uk/Conditions/pregnancy-and-baby/Pages/making-up-infant-formula.aspx#close

Expressing
www.netmums.com/baby/feeding-your-new-baby/how-to-express-with-success

CHAPTER 4 - KEEPING YOUR TODDLER OCCUPIED

Baby proofing your home
www.babycentre.co.uk/a460/making-your-home-safe-for-your-baby

First-born jealousy
http://www.pantley.com/files/FirstBornJealousy.pdf

CHAPTER 5 - GETTING OUT OF THE HOUSE

Renting double buggies
http://www.rentabuggy.co.uk

Sling libraries
http://ukslinglibraries.wordpress.com

Safe baby wearing
www.babywearinginternational.org/pages/safety.php

Rear-facing car seats
www.rearfacing.co.uk

CHAPTER 6 - SCHEDULE OR GO WITH THE FLOW?

More on scheduling and types of routines
www.babycenter.com/0_the-basics-of-baby-schedules-why-when-and-how-to-start-a-rou_3658352.bc?page=1

Attachment parenting
www.attachmentparenting.org

CHAPTER 7 - BATH AND BEDTIME

Storing your child's artwork electronically
www.artkiveapp.com

www.mykidsartbook.wordpress.com

This book has been written with the help and support of MumPanel, UK-based mum marketing and insight specialists...

Sign up to MumPanel, give your opinions in surveys, focus groups and by testing products. Let brands know what mums really want with chances to win £100s of Love2shop vouchers.

www.mumpanel.co.uk

THE CENTRAL YMCA GUIDES SERIES

Happy and Healthy: A collection of trustworthy advice on health, fitness and wellbeing topics

UK
http://www.centralymcaguides.com/hhct2

US
http://www.centralymcaguides.com/hhct

The Scientific Approach to Exercise for Fat Loss: How to get in shape and shed unwanted fat by using healthy and scientifically proven techniques

UK
http://www.centralymcaguides.com/sael2

US
http://www.centralymcaguides.com/sael

The Need to Know Guide to Nutrition for Exercise: How your food and drink can help you to achieve your workout goals

UK
http://www.centralymcaguides.com/ngne2

US
http://www.centralymcaguides.com/ngne

The Need to Know Guide to Nutrition and Healthy Eating: The perfect starter to eating well or how to eat the right foods, stay in shape and stick to a healthy diet

UK
http://www.centralymcaguides.com/gnhe2

US http://www.centralymcaguides.com/gnhe

Tri Harder - The A to Z of Triathlon for Improvers: The triathlon competitors' guide to training and improving your running, cycling and swimming times

UK
http://www.centralymcaguides.com/thtc2

US http://www.centralymcaguides.com/thtc

20 Full Body Training Programmes for Exercise Lovers: An essential guide to boosting your general fitness, strength, power and endurance

UK http://www.centralymcaguides.com/tpel2

US http://www.centralymcaguides.com/tpel

Run, Jump, Climb, Crawl: The essential training guide for obstacle racing enthusiasts, or how to get fit, stay safe and prepare for the toughest mud runs on the planet

UK
http://www.centralymcaguides.com/rjc2

US
http://www.centralymcaguides.com/rjc

Gardening for Health: The Need to Know Guide to the Health Benefits of Horticulture

UK
http://www.centralymcaguides.com/gfhh2

US
http://www.centralymcaguides.com/gfhh

New Baby, New You: The Need to Know Guide to Postnatal Health and Happiness - How to return to exercise and get back in shape after giving birth

UK
http://www.centralymcaguides.com/nbny2

US
http://www.centralymcaguides.com/nbny

The Need to Know Guide to Life with a Toddler and a Newborn: How to prepare for and cope with the day to day challenge of raising two young children

UK
http://www.centralymcaguides.com/ngtn2

US
http://www.centralymcaguides.com/ngtn

50 Games for Active Toddlers: Quick everyday hints and tips to keep toddlers active, healthy and occupied

UK
http://www.centralymcaguides.com/50uk

US
http://www.centralymcaguides.com/50us

Exercise and Nutrition 3 Book Bundle

UK
http://www.centralymcaguides.com/enb2

US
http://www.centralymcaguides.com/enb

Obstacle Racing Preparation 3 Book Bundle

UK
http://www.centralymcaguides.com/orpb2

US
http://www.centralymcaguides.com/orpb

Nutrition and Fat Loss 3 Book Bundle

UK
http://www.centralymcaguides.com/nflb2

US
http://www.centralymcaguides.com/nflb

Mums' Health 3 Book Bundle

UK
http://www.centralymcaguides.com/mhb2

US
http://www.centralymcaguides.com/mhb

Discover more books and ebooks of interest to you and find out about the range of work we do at the forefront of health, fitness and wellbeing.

www.centralymcaguides.com

Printed in Great Britain
by Amazon.co.uk, Ltd.,
Marston Gate.